FUN FACTS

Ripley's Believe It or Not!® Kids

& SILLY STORIES

ACTIVITY ANNUAL 2018

Ripley PUBLISHING

a Jim Pattison Company

What's Inside

消火栓

CHECK THIS OUT!

Bonedigger the lion at the G.W. Exotic Animal Park in Wynnewood, Oklahoma, USA, has a pack of doggy friends! Dachshunds Milo, Bullet and Angel have comforted the disabled lion since he was just a cub.

Beast Friends

After seeing how well the dogs got along with Bonedigger, their handler, John Reinke, introduced them to other big cats.

Lions that don't belong to a pride are called 'nomads'.

Male lions in Tsavo, Kenya, don't have manes!

Lions are the only cats with manes.

5

Bee-lieve it or not, bees come in colours other than yellow and black!

Orchid Bees

They are found mostly in Central and South America, have extremely long tongues and don't live in a hive.

Orchid bees can be blue, purple, red, orange and green!

Under the BIG TOP

Find all 16 terms hidden in the circus tent! Make sure to look up, down, backward, across and diagonally!

acrobat

sideshow

balloon

tightrope

magician

unicycle

applause

strongman

fun house

bumper cars

big top

candy

arena

animals

clowns

trapeze

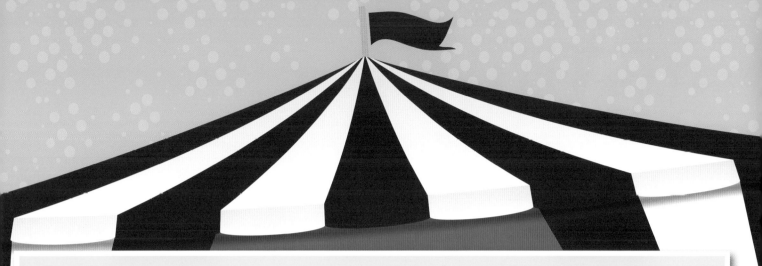

```
a p p l a u s e j t j c u j x n m t t f
q h f r u l i s h d a n d s u a g a z u
e s u o h l d n l n q i g x d m a y j n
m i y p y e e d a o w o r e g r d a h
k m y o u r s y t x m e n z h n e h j o
h k a t n d h s g s v i e p k o n q l u
m v r g v z o p z w m p n j w r a b u s
b d s i i k w n b l a q e a n t x y h e
o m j b j c y t x r b o z i t s r h q p
l q y t r u i b t x e t a m b j m p q e
t a b o r c a a s a f u n e r e n n k e
n s w w j m s x n i q q m g p t u o a f
l k c r w a g o f g a w b o v n b o u r
h f p l y n t v j u s z r a i y u l y y
p o r w o w w d b s f t r c z t e l t x
t n k n j w c c n o h l y p t c g a e c
b y m q e r n r p g b c l v x a e b a n
z j n x l f m s i w l g b g t g f r h m
k x i i b t k e l u b d x l q z z z
v u u w j a z b s r a c r e p m u b v w
```

Want to see how you did?
Turn to pages 88-90 for the solutions!

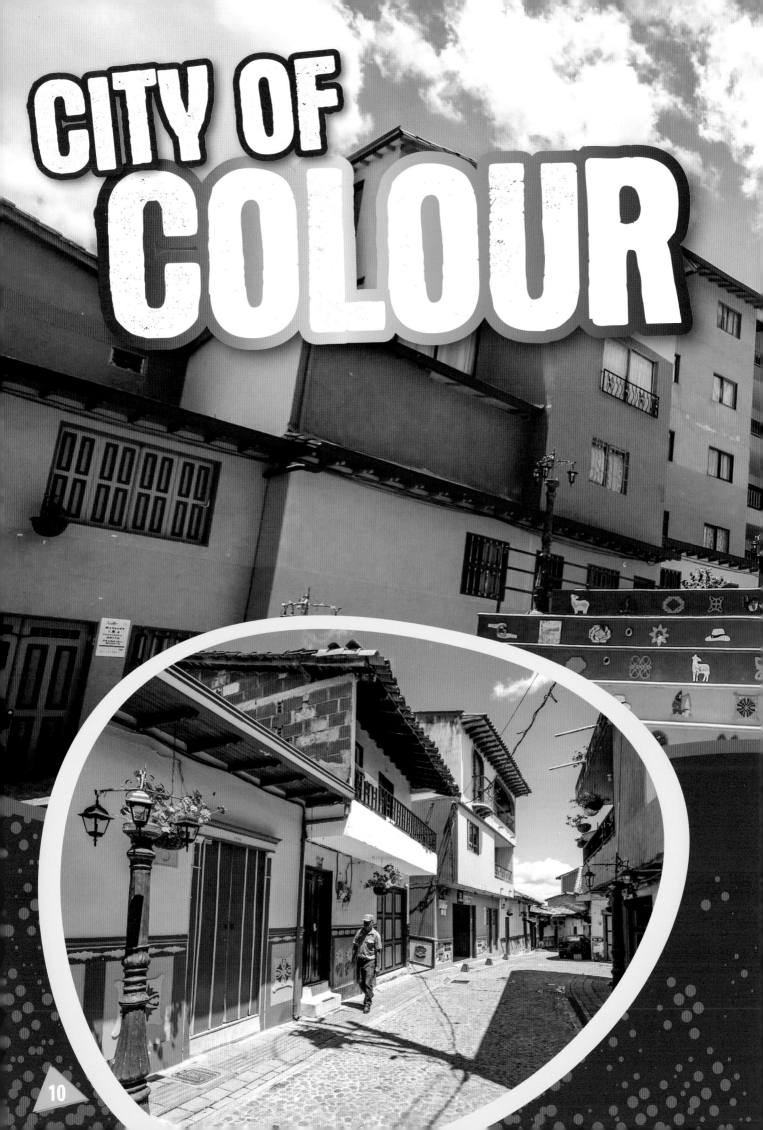

CITY OF COLOUR

Stunning colour dazzles the eye in the small town of Guatapé, Colombia! Most of this town – from walls and doors to balconies and steps – is painted in bright, vibrant colours!

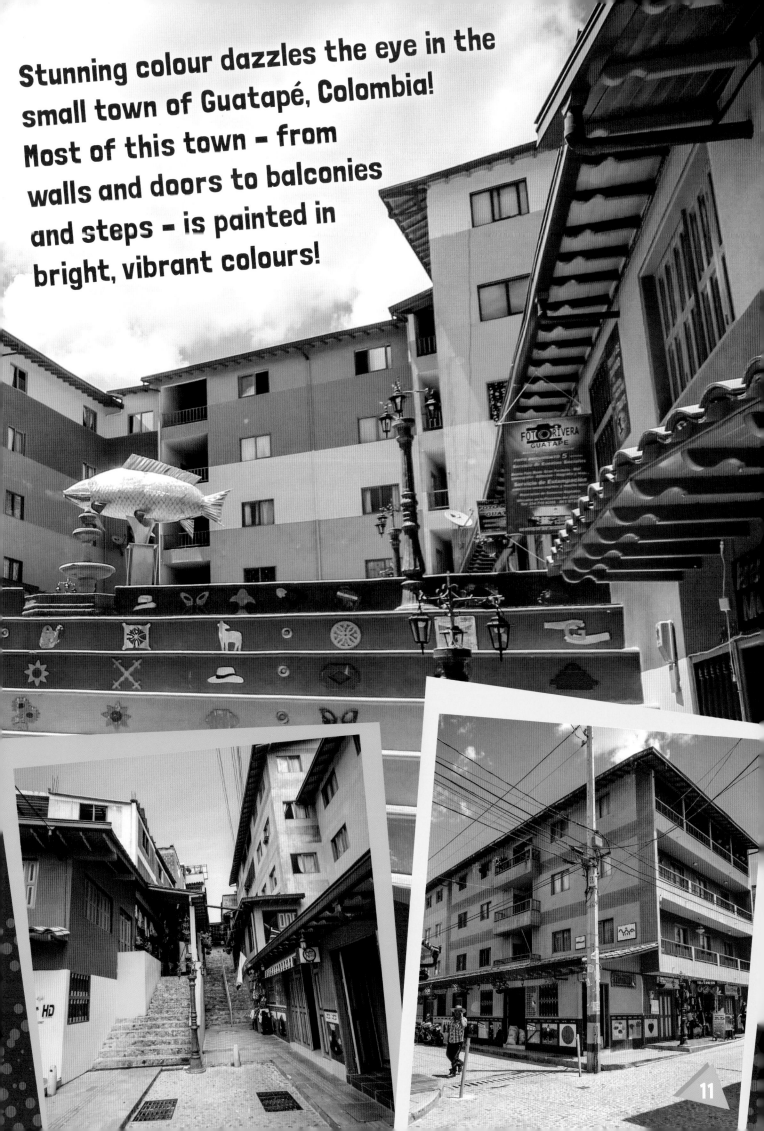

All about Jellies...

Scientists have merged jelly and feline DNA to create glow-in-the-dark cats!

Jellies eat fish, shrimp, crabs and tiny plants.

Jellies existed before dinosaurs.

Jellies have no bones, hearts or brains.

Jellies are 95 per cent water.

Some sea turtles eat jellies.

Under the Sea

Take turns with your friends and choose words to fill in the blanks – the sillier, the better! After you are done, read it out loud!

Today _____ and I went scuba diving in the ocean near _____ !
    person   **noun**

The weather was _____ , not a _____ in the sky. Our guide
    adjective   **noun**

_____ us into our _____ and then we were on our way! The
verb ending in -ed   **noun**

water was a little _____ , but we could see so many _____ .
    adjective   **noun**

Besides all the _____ fish, we saw _____ , _____
    adjective   **plural noun**   **plural noun**

and even a _____ _____ ! I thought it would be loud
    adjective   **singular noun**

underwater, but it was so _____ . I was a little _____ when
    adjective   **verb ending in -ed**

_____ swam by, though. Our guide made sure we _____ away
    noun   **verb ending in -ed**

from the _____ so we stayed safe. I hope we can do this again soon.
    noun

Cute but Deadly

Every year, moose actually attack more people than bears.

The bite of a tiny blue-ringed octopus can kill an adult human within minutes.

The adorable slow loris secretes poison from its elbows.

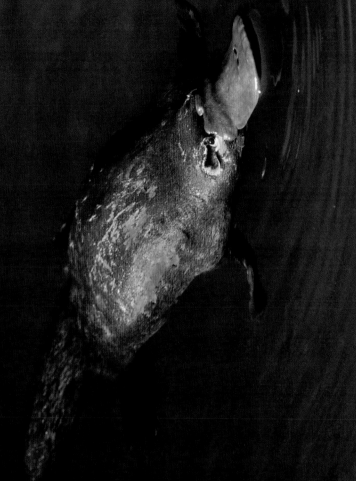

The adult male platypus has a venomous pointed spur above the heel of each hind leg.

Pufferfish poison is very potent and can easily kill by paralysing the diaphragm, causing suffocation.

When disturbed, the flightless cassowary bird of Australia and New Guinea is capable of using its large claws to disembowel its attacker.

Food curators Miss Cakehead and the Tattooed Bakers once created a life-size unicorn cake! The tasteful creature was filled with rainbow-coloured cake layers.

Hungry for More

Farmer Andrew Burgess of Peterborough, England, created hybrid cauliflowers in different colours!

The Hamdog is a crazy combination of a hot dog and hamburger. The hot dog sits between a sliced burger inside a specially designed bun.

19

Strange Slices

Pizza is enjoyed all across the globe, but it's not always prepared in familiar ways. Check out how these countries like to top their pizza!

Costa Rica
coconut
shrimp
pineapple

21

One Foot Wander

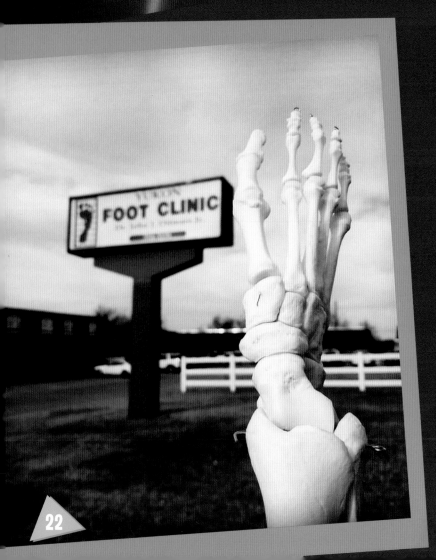

After being diagnosed with cancer, Kristi Loyall of Oklahoma, USA, was forced to amputate her right foot - but decided to keep it! She started the Instagram account @onefootwander, showing her cleaned, whitened foot posing in funny situations.

We had a chat with Kristi and her funny bone.

....

Q: What gave you the idea to keep your foot after the amputation?

A: When my doctor told me amputation would be the best option, the first thing I asked was if I could have my foot back. One of my coping mechanisms is to make a joke out of things, so that's what I was trying to do, and then I realised I really did want my foot back.

Q: Did you name your foot? If so, what's its name?

A: Sometimes I call it Footzilla, but the actual name I came up with is Achilles.

Q: What kind of reactions do you get when you are out with your foot?

A: I think most people assume it's fake when they see it. No one has ever really commented on it while I was taking photos. One time when I was at a drive-thru, the cashier saw my best friend holding it and said, 'I like your foot', and I thought, 'Haha, if only you knew'.

The Hulk was originally grey in colour, but Marvel changed him to green after problems with the ink.

The Library of Congress, USA, has the world's largest comic book collection. They currently have more than 100,000 individual issues.

Superman once wielded Thor's hammer.

Spider-Man has a hyphen in his name so that people don't confuse him with Superman.

Super Facts

25

Hidden Heroes

Find all 16 superheroes hidden in disguise! Make sure to look up, down, backward, across and diagonally!

Spider-Man

Iron Man

Superman

Captain America

Green Arrow

Thor

Flash

Batman

Wolverine

Aquaman

Hulk

Professor X

Wonder Woman

Doctor Strange

Wasp

Black Panther

BONUS! Find the hidden villain in this puzzle. Write the villain's name here:

_____ !

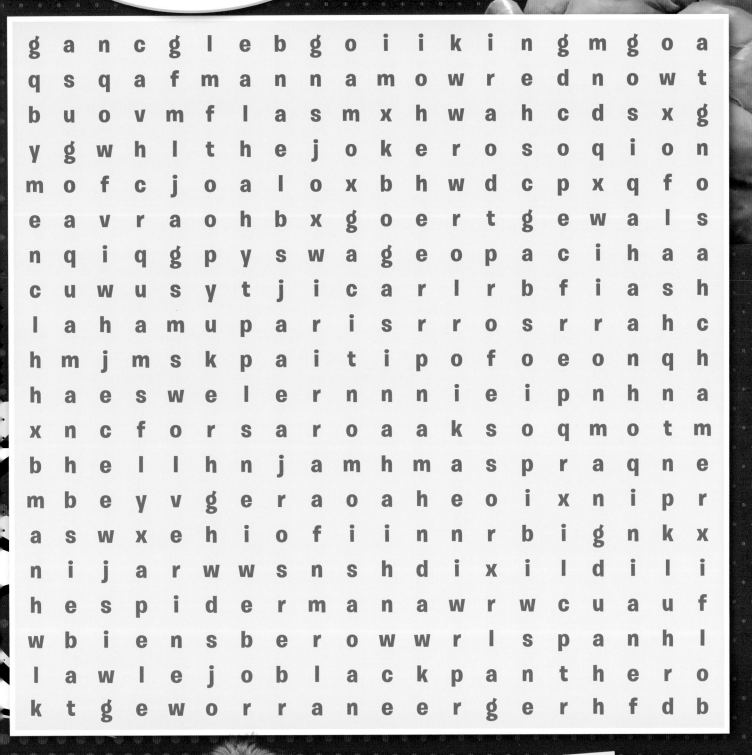

g a n c g l e b g o i i k i n g m g o a
q s q a f m a n n a m o w r e d n o w t
b u o v m f l a s m x h w a h c d s x g
y g w h l t h e j o k e r o s o q i o n
m o f c j o a l o x b h w d c p x q f o
e a v r a o h b x g o e r t g e w a l s
n q i q g p y s w a g e o p a c i h a a
c u w u s y t j i c a r l r b f i a s h
l a h a m u p a r i s r r o s r r a h c
h m j m s k p a i t i p o f o e o n q h
h a e s w e l e r n n n i e i p n h n a
x n c f o r s a r o a a k s o q m o t m
b h e l l h n j a m h m a s p r a q n e
m b e y v g e r a o a h e o i x n i p r
a s w x e h i o f i i n n r b i g n k x
n i j a r w w s n s h d i x i l d i l i
h e s p i d e r m a n a w r w c u a u f
w b i e n s b e r o w w r l s p a n h l
l a w l e j o b l a c k p a n t h e r o
k t g e w o r r a n e e r g e r h f d b

Want to see how you did?
Turn to pages 88-90 for the solutions!

Despite their name, sun bears are nocturnal.

Kodiak bear cubs weigh less than a pound when born, but grow to be one of the largest bears in the world.

Bear with Us!

Sloth bears will put their mouths over insect nests and suck up bugs through a gap in their front teeth.

Giant pandas have an extra large bone on their paws specifically for holding bamboo.

Black bears can be black, brown, cinnamon, blonde, blue-grey or white.

Polar bears are the only carnivorous bear species; all others are omnivores.

tigers

bats

gators

Gather 'Round

wombats

rhinos

squirrels

dolphins

Draw a line to connect the name of each animal with its group name.

cauldron   congregation

flamboyance   crash

wisdom   scurry

streak   pod

tribe   pride

lions

goats

flamingos

Want to see how you did?
Turn to pages 88-90 for the solutions!

It's Going Down

Looking up from below Trifonov's balloon

Austrian pilot Ivan Trifonov successfully landed a hot-air balloon in the 206-metre deep Mamet Cave in Croatia.

Zip World transformed an old mine in Blaenau Ffestiniog, North Wales, into Bounce Below – six levels of bouncy nets more than 30 metres above the cavern floor!

Bride Alexandra and groom Mikhail shot their wedding photos 100 metres belowground in an abandoned mineshaft in Chelyabinskaya Oblast, Russia!

Sianagh Gallagher dominates the rock climbing wall despite being born with no arm, collarbone or shoulder blade on the left side of her body.

Rock the WALL

The York native is captain of the Great Britain Paraclimbing Team, whose members are all differently abled athletes.

Mountain Slide

Rodelbahn alpine roller coasters race through hundreds of metres of the Swiss Alps. Riders travel in a wheeled toboggan while controlling their own speed with a cart-mounted brake and must slow themselves down to keep from toppling over on turns.

Follow the slides to find out which team makes it to the bottom without taking a detour!

FINISH

Want to see how you did?
Turn to pages 88-90 for the solutions!

Sporty Animals

I want to be like Hawkeye!

Hawkeye the cat went on more than 20 underwater trips after her owner, Gene Alba of Redding, California, USA, built her a custom scuba suit!

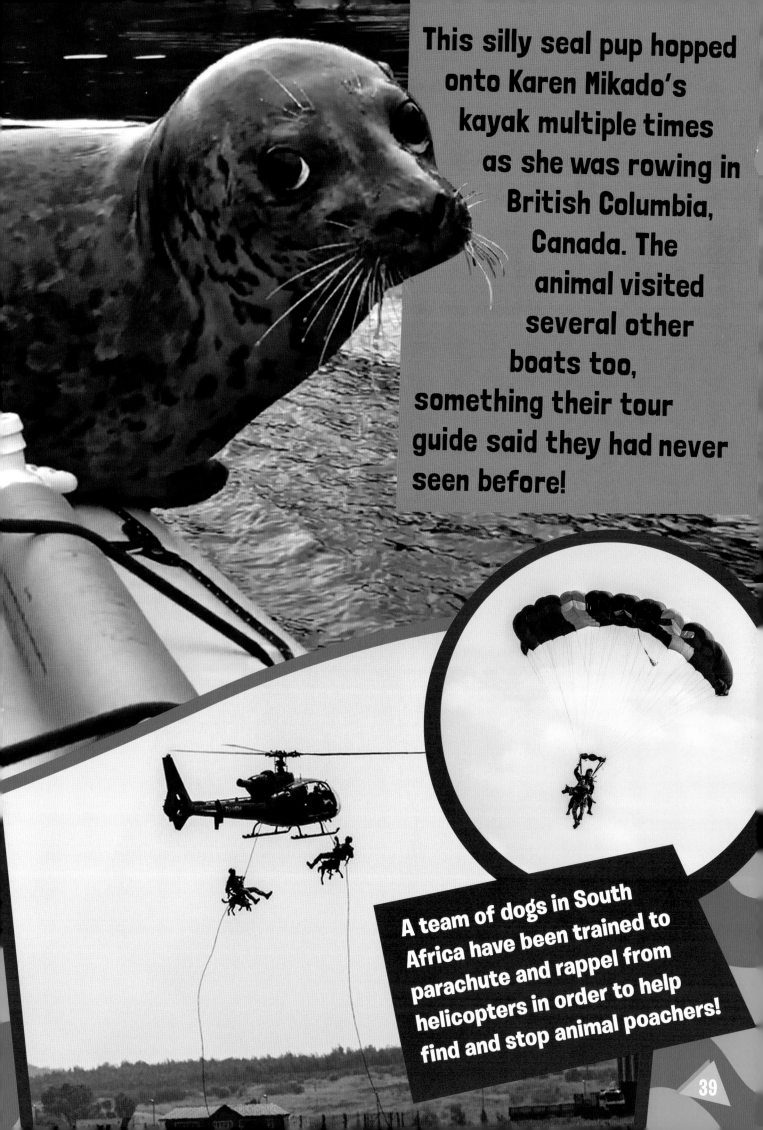

This silly seal pup hopped onto Karen Mikado's kayak multiple times as she was rowing in British Columbia, Canada. The animal visited several other boats too, something their tour guide said they had never seen before!

A team of dogs in South Africa have been trained to parachute and rappel from helicopters in order to help find and stop animal poachers!

NOIX DE VIE

RATIGAN
EUROPEAN TOUR 2017

AUS
EXHIBITION
GALERI IWERKS
NOV - 19 JAN

RENEGADES

84-16
New Album

VÄNNA INGET

TORS 15 DECEMBER

NO TIME
FOR US

KENT

LITTLE SHOP of Cheeses

An unknown artist called Anonymouse
opened secret mice-sized shops
hidden in the city of Malmö, Sweden!

Although the artist is a mystery, these tiny shops for mice offer nuts, cheese and a cosy atmosphere.

Dry weather conditions in 2014 made it difficult for wild hedgehogs in the UK to get ready for hibernation.

Hedgehog

I'm looking pretty sharp today!

To help the small animals, home improvement store B&Q teamed up with the Wildlife Aid Foundation to create this hedgehog-sized 'drive-thru'!

MENU
SNAILS
SLUGS
MEALWORMS
CENTIPEDES

OPEN

TODAY'S SPECIALS

FRESH BEETLES

DRIVE THROUGH

Drive-Thru

It's filled with yummy bugs for the prickly creatures to eat!

DRIVE T

Desert DOTS

Connect the dots to see what desert animals are in the oasis.

START 1
2
75
3
8
9
7
10
74
4 5 6
73
11
68 69
70
72
12
66 67
71
13
64 65
63
62
49
14
61
15
60
16
59
51 50
17
58
48 40
31
30
23 22
52
41 39
21
57
47 42
32
29 24
18
56
54
38
20
43
28 25
53
37 33
55
46
27 26
19
45 44 36 34
35

44

Terry Taylor from Essex feeds wild robins, putting a worm between his lips for them to nab.

For the Birds

Made from the spit of the cave-dwelling swiftlet bird, these nests are used to make soup and can cost thousands of pounds per kilogram!

Chinese New Year

Did you know? A Chinese New Year tradition is to give red envelopes filled with money.

YUE HWA
CHINESE PRODUCTS

Each year is associated with a zodiac animal:

Rat	Rabbit	Horse	Rooster
Ox	Dragon	Goat	Dog
Tiger	Snake	Monkey	Pig

Chinese New Year, also known as the Spring Festival, is the most important holiday in China. Between January and February, families come together to rest, eat, celebrate a year of hard work and wish for a lucky and prosperous new year.

An electric eel is not an eel at all, but a type of knifefish.

Despite its name, the bearcat is not closely related to bears or cats.

Hippopotamus literally means 'river horse' in Greek.

The elephant shrew is more closely related to elephants than shrews.

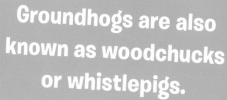

Groundhogs are also known as woodchucks or whistlepigs.

What's in a Name?

Wait... What?

A group of frogs is called an army.

Early explorers in Antarctica classified penguins as fish.

PB & Worm Cookies

Stuff you need:

- 225 grams earthworms
- 240 ml peanut butter
- 240 ml sugar
- 1 teaspoon vanilla
- 1 egg
- 240 ml flour

1. Boil earthworms for 10 minutes and drain.
2. Mix all ingredients together.
3. Divide dough into balls and place 2.5 centimetres apart on an ungreased baking tray.
4. Bake 12 to 15 minutes at 180°C.

Feeling a little grossed out? Substitute creepy crawlies with sweets! Use 12 Strawberry Laces to replace the worms. Skipping step 1, prepare as instructed, and while cookies are still hot, place your sweet worms on top!

It is commonplace in parts of Africa, Latin America and Southeast Asia to eat insects. You may not realize it, but you eat about 400–900 grams of insects each year - bits and pieces of them sneak into your food!

There are nearly 2,000 types of edible insects on Earth!

ENTOMOPHAGY

(ˌen(t)əˈmäfəjē/)

: noun

The practice of eating insects.

In ancient Greece, cicadas were a fancy snack!

What's in the Water?

Alien-like feather stars are marine invertebrates with arms that have feathery fringes used for swimming.

The cute ribbon seal (*Histriophoca fasciata*) is patterned with four white bands and can be found in the icy waters off Russia's southern coast and north of Korea and Japan.

The blobfish might not look so flabby and gross when at home, since deep sea pressure gives their bodies structural support.

Ice World

Fill in the blanks with the correct Antarctic or Arctic animal. Then order the numbered letters to reveal the secret message!

(1) I have thick, white fur and strong paws to catch seals.

___ ___ ___ ___ ___ ___ ___
   21   7   3

(2) I'm a bird that can't fly, but I can swim!

___ ___ ___ ___ ___ ___ ___
   12 9 15   16

(3) I'm known as the unicorn of the sea.

___ ___ ___ ___ ___ ___ ___ ___
18   14 1 10   4

(4) I have two long tusks and a whole lot of blubber.

___ ___ ___ ___ ___ ___
22   5   8 19

(5) I help Santa pull his sleigh!

___ ___ ___ ___ ___ ___ ___
   17 20 13

(6) I'm a small, white whale with a big head.

___ ___ ___ ___ ___
 2 6   11

SECRET MESSAGE:

___ ___ ___ ___ ___ ___ ___ ___ ___ ___ ___ ___ ___   ___ ___ ___   ___ ___   ___ ___ ___ ___ !
1 2 3 4 5 6 7 8 9 10 11 12 13 14 15 16 17 18 19 20 21 22

Help the orca calf find her way back to her pod!

Want to see how you did?
Turn to pages 88-90 for the solutions!

Batty Batfish

The red-lipped batfish lives in the waters around the Galápagos Islands, and it walks on the ocean floor with its lower fins!

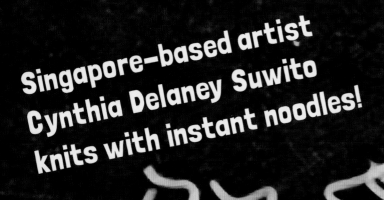

Singapore—based artist Cynthia Delaney Suwito knits with instant noodles!

Knitting Noodles

Cynthia sees instant noodles as something that people find comfort in because they are quick and easy. To help people slow down, she takes what is 'instant' and makes it time-consuming.

We talked with Cynthia to help unravel some answers.

Q: Why did you decide to knit instant noodles?

A: I realized that instant noodles look like threads, and it was a natural reaction to start wanting to knit with them.

Q: How is knitting noodles different from knitting yarn?

A: Knitting with instant noodles is more difficult, and it takes more time. Noodles break easily and cannot be joined together. It took me one day to learn how to knit yarn, but knitting instant noodles took me months of practice.

Q: How big is the finished piece, or are you constantly adding to it?

A: It is currently 12 centimetres wide and 1.5 metres long, but I am going to add to it to make it longer.

More than 171 million Americans celebrated Halloween in 2016.

Jack-o'-lanterns originated in Ireland, but since they didn't have access to pumpkins, they would carve turnips and swedes.

For Halloween 2016, some of our divers at the Ripley's Aquarium in Gatlinburg, Tennessee, USA, carved pumpkins underwater in our Shark Lagoon!

Trick or Treat Yourself

At many pumpkin festivals, people make huge pumpkin pyramids containing thousands of gourds that stretch up high into the air!

GOURD
(gôrd, goord)

: noun
A gourd is a fleshy, typically large fruit with a hard skin, some varieties of which are edible.

Halloween Fun!

Germany's Ludwigsburg Castle hosts an annual giant pumpkin boat race in the former royal palace's massive fountain!

Give this jack-o'-lantern a scary face!

Draw the rectangles in the correct order to reveal the spooky picture.

Want to see how you did?
Turn to pages 88-90 for the solutions!

6

12

2

10

4

1

3

8

TRICK OR

11

TREAT   TREAT

5

9

7

1

2

3

4

5

6

7

8

9

10

11

12

Visitors to Gumeracha, Australia, can climb the world's biggest rocking horse at the Toy Factory!

Barbie's actual full name is Barbara Millicent Roberts.

There are 43 quintillion possible Rubik's cube combinations.

68

Toyland

Using more than three million bricks, former *Top Gear* host James May and the BBC built a LEGO house in 2009! It even featured a flushable toilet.

The first version of Minecraft was created in just six days.

All cows in Minecraft are female, since they can all give out milk.

Minecraft

One of Minecraft's stranger native species, the creeper, actually began as a coding error.

If Minecraft were real, one Minecraft block in real life would equal 1 m³. That means the Minecraft world is bigger than some planets.

The creator's personal Minecraft avatar is the only game resident who drops an apple when he dies.

One in every 10,000 times you play the game, its introductory menu will flash a misspelling of the title, reversing the 'E' and the 'C' to read 'Minceraft'.

The Enderman language is actually English in reverse (and at a lower pitch).

71

Manhole Art

Manhole covers in Japan feature kawaii, or cute, designs!

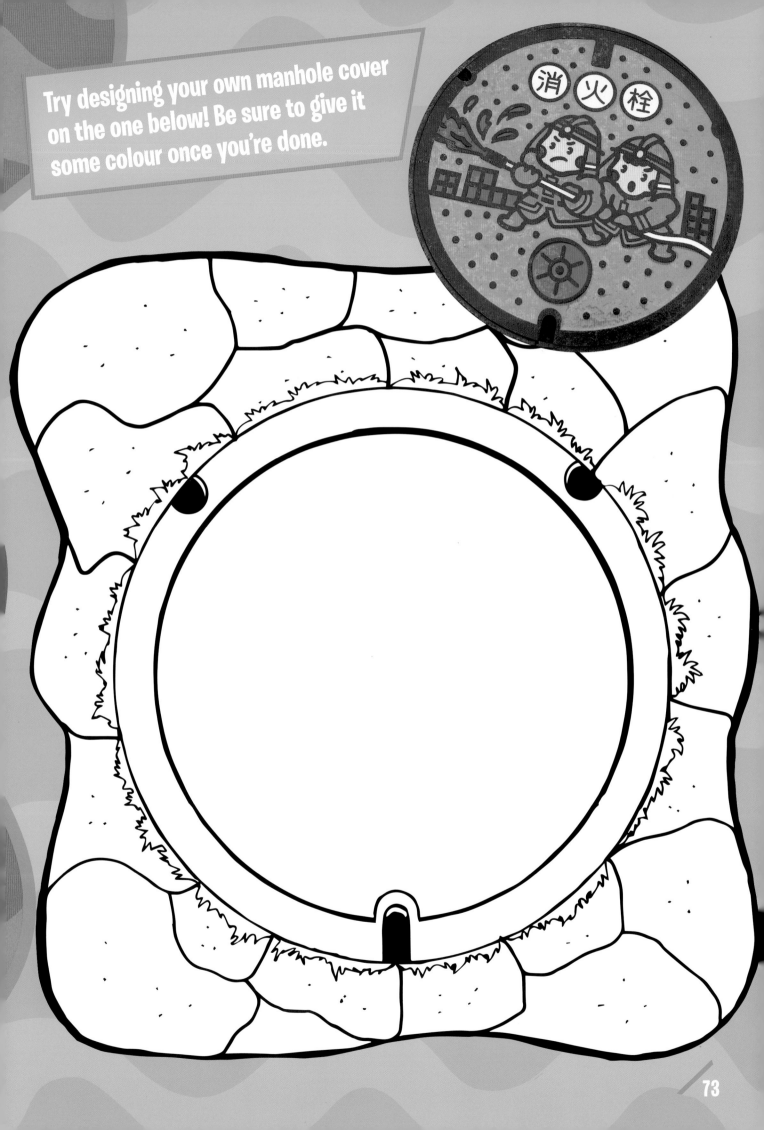

Try designing your own manhole cover on the one below! Be sure to give it some colour once you're done.

Kooky Kiwis

Kiwi birds are only found in New Zealand, and are the national symbol of the country.

About the size of a chicken, kiwis are flightless birds with a long beak.

They got their name from the sound of their calls, making 'kee-wee, kee-wee' noises.

Unlike other birds, kiwi chicks are already covered in feathers as soon as they hatch.

'Kiwi' is a nickname for people from New Zealand.

Kiwi fruit was named after the kiwi bird because they are both small, brown and furry.

Kiwi fruits are actually native to China.

The brown fuzz on kiwi fruit is actually edible!

Blast from the Past

When she met Mark Antony, Cleopatra is said to have arrived on a golden barge rowed by oars made of silver, while attendants dressed as cupids fanned her.

Pope Benedict IX was the youngest pope ever, between 12 and 20 years old when he started his rule.

In 2012, a couple invited the Queen to their wedding as a joke, and she turned up.

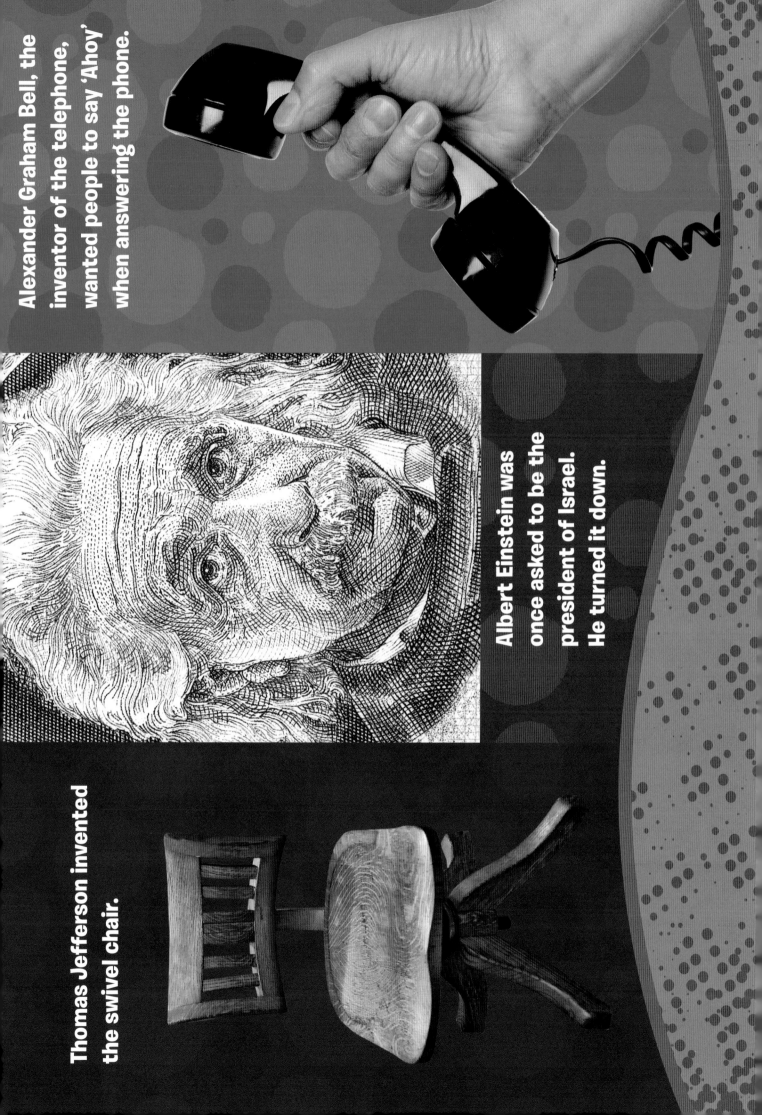

Alexander Graham Bell, the inventor of the telephone, wanted people to say 'Ahoy' when answering the phone.

Albert Einstein was once asked to be the president of Israel. He turned it down.

Thomas Jefferson invented the swivel chair.

Cool! Calligraphy

Thousands gather in Tokyo, Japan, every January to ring in the new year with a calligraphy contest, writing out resolutions, poems and other phrases.

Can You Kanji?

These two characters, or symbols, mean 'Happy New Year' in kanji!

KANJI

(ˌkän-(ˈ)jē)

: noun

A Japanese writing system with symbols that represent whole ideas rather than individual sounds.

In Japan, hanko, or stamps, are used in place of signatures. Artists can customise their hanko by having their last name or a favourite word or phrase carved on their seal.

賀春

Follow the numbered steps to the left and try your hand at writing this Japanese New Year's greeting in kanji. Then, sign it with your own hanko design in the red square!

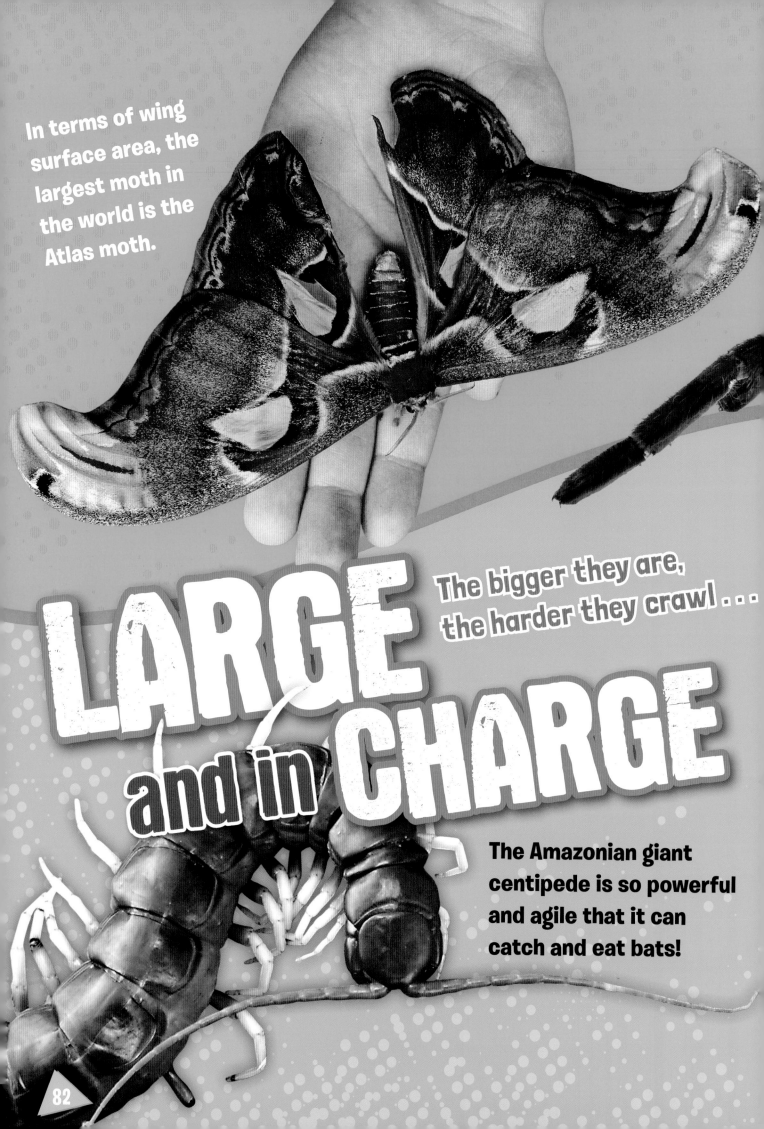

In terms of wing surface area, the largest moth in the world is the Atlas moth.

The bigger they are, the harder they crawl . . .

LARGE and in CHARGE

The Amazonian giant centipede is so powerful and agile that it can catch and eat bats!

The goliath birdeater tarantula of South America is the biggest spider in the world!

Its legs can span up to 30 centimetres wide!

Found in South America, the titan beetle is a giant! Their mouthparts, or mandibles, are so strong they can snap wooden pencils in half!

Luke Skywalker's lightsaber flew into space aboard the space shuttle *Discovery*.

While filming *Star Wars* in the Pacific Northwest, USA, Chewbacca actor Peter Mayhew had bodyguards to protect him from bigfoot hunters.

Water Wars

Devin Graham and the Supertramp film crew modified Jetovator watercrafts to recreate the speeder bike scene in *Return of the Jedi*. Most of the modifications were accomplished with duct tape!

Flying High

Follow the path to find out which numbered net Zazel lands in.

START HERE

1

2

3

4

Want to see how you did?
Turn to pages 88-90 for the solutions!

The first recorded human cannonball was a 14-year-old girl - acrobat Rosa 'Zazel' Richter - who was shot 9 metres into the air in London in 1877.

P O S S I B L E

3 letters
net
air
fly

4 letters
girl
high
bold
bang
exit

5 letters
human
Zazel
brave
stunt
first

6 letters
safety
steady
launch

7 letters
acrobat
ability
strange
pioneer

8 letters
possible
athletic
dramatic
momentum
dizzying

9 letters
daredevil
dangerous
entertain

10 letters
cannonball

Using the word bank, write the words on the criss-cross grid. We've placed one word to get you started!

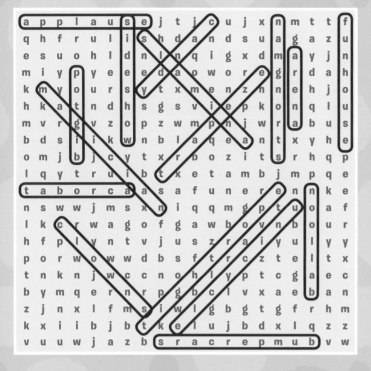

Gather 'Round, page 30–31

Streak = Tigers   **Flamingos = Flamboyance**

Bats = Cauldron   **Goats = Tribe**

Squirrels = Scurry   **Rhinos = Crash**

Dolphins = Pod   **Wombats = Wisdom**

Lions = Pride   **Gators = Congregation**

Mountain Slide, page 37

FINISH

Year-End Round-Up, page 50

Year-End Round-Up, page 51

HAPPY NEW YEAR

Yawn	Pray
Hyper	Repay
Paper	Payer
Earn	Hyena
Near	Happen
Napper	Anyway

Ice World, page 58

Ice World, page 59

1. I have thick, white fur and strong paws to catch seals.

2. I'm a bird that can't fly, but I can swim!

3. I'm known as the unicorn of the sea.

4. I have two long tusks and a whole lot of blubber.

5. I help Santa pull his sleigh!

6. I'm a small, white whale with a big head.

P O L A R   B E A R
21   7   3

P E N G U I N
12   9   15   16

N A R W H A L
18   14   1   10   4

W A L R U S
22   5   8   19

R E I N D E E R
17   20   13

B E L U G A
2   6   11

SECRET MESSAGE:

W E   A L L   L A U G H   A N D   R U N   I N   S N O W !
1   2   3   4   5   6   7   8   9   10   11   12   13   14   15   16   17   18   19   20   21   22

Halloween Fun, page 67

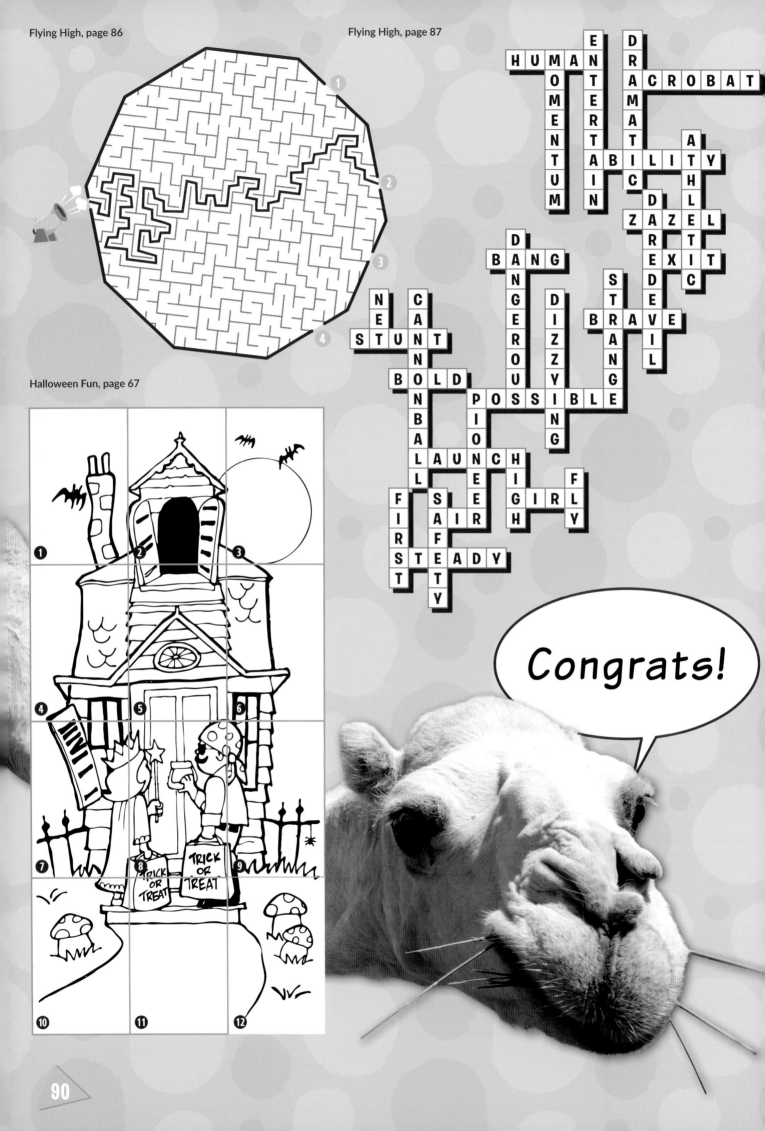

Congrats!

ABC's and 123's

Share some silliness and fun as little ones learn their ABC's and 123's. Filled with wacky, wonderful characters and sweet illustrations, they'll enjoy counting and saying their alphabet again and again!

FUN FACTS & SILLY STORIES

Filled with wacky stories and colorful images of crazy animals, incredible talents, amazing people and goofy events, readers will have a hard time putting these books down!

If you have a fun fact or a silly story, email it to us at bionresearch@ripleys.com

OTHER TITLES IN THIS SERIES

Featuring brand new Believe It or Not! stories, puzzles and games, Ripley's fans are guaranteed to giggle and gasp their way through these books!

THE BIG ONE!

ONE ZANY DAY!

ODD AROUND THE WORLD!

ACKNOWLEDGEMENTS

FRONT COVER © Andrew Lam/Shutterstock.com; **BACK COVER** (tr) © David Aleksandrowicz/Shutterstock.com, (bl) © Kawin K/Shutterstock.com; **IFC** © KengComp/Shutterstock.com; **2** (tl) © livcool/Shutterstock.com, (tr) blickwinkel/Alamy Stock Photo, (bl) © Tikhonov/Shutterstock.com; **2–3** (b) Courtesy of Mark Murray; **3** (tr) Kristi Loyall, @onefootwander, (br) © FUN FUN PHOTO/Shutterstock.com; **4** Barcroft USA; **5** (tr) © Steffen Foerster/Shutterstock.com, (b) © holbox/Shutterstock.com; **6–7** Nature Collection/Alamy Stock Photo; **8** (tr) © YAKOBCHUK VIACHESLAV/Shutterstock.com, (b) © volodyar/Shutterstock.com; **9** © Kolonko/Shutterstock.com; **10–11** Jessica Devnani/Media Drum World/Caters News; **12–13** (bkg) © KengComp/Shutterstock.com, (b) © AnnaSimo/Shutterstock.com; **14–15** © Jag_cz/Shutterstock.com; **16** (t) © Pictureguy/Shutterstock.com, (cr) © Teguh Tirtaputra/Shutterstock.com, (br) © Seregraff/Shutterstock.com; **17** (tl) © worldswildlifewonders/Shutterstock.com, (tr) © Boligolov Andrew/Shutterstock.com, (br) © Sanit Fuangnakhon/Shutterstock.com; **18** Tattooed Bakers www.tattooedbakers.com. Image by Baker and Maker; **19** (t) Bournemouth News/REX/Shutterstock, (bl) Courtesy of Mark Murray; **20–21** (bkg) © Artem Shadrin/Shutterstock.com; **22–23** Kristi Loyall, @onefootwander; **24** (tl) © StevePhotos/Shutterstock.com, (tr) © Irina Levitskaya/Shutterstock.com, (bl) © lacostique/Shutterstock.com, (bc) © Irina Levitskaya/Shutterstock.com; **24–25** © FUN FUN PHOTO/Shutterstock.com; **25** (tr) © SunshineVector/Shutterstock.com; **26** (tr) © Sarunyu L/Shutterstock.com, (b) © NoraVector/Shutterstock.com; **27** (tr) © Sarunyu L/Shutterstock.com; **28** (br) © SKARIDA/Shutterstock.com; **28–29** (bkg) © Zhou Eka/Shutterstock.com; **29** (bl) © AF studio/Shutterstock.com, (br) © Olga Lebedeva/Shutterstock.com; **30** (tl) © Serjio74/Shutterstock.com, (tr) © tanaphongpict/Shutterstock.com, (cl) © Rudy Umans/Shutterstock.com, (bl) © Gekko Gallery/Shutterstock.com, (br) © Chris Price at PulseFoto/Shutterstock.com; **31** (tl) © geertweggen/Shutterstock.com, (tr) © Chase Dekker/Shutterstock.com, (cr) © Foto Mous/Shutterstock.com, (bl) © remore/Shutterstock.com, (br) © Anton_Ivanov/Shutterstock.com; **32** (l) Haron Markičević/MERCURY PRESS/CATERS NEWS; **32–33** Zip World UK; **33** (cr) CATERS NEWS; **34** Jim McAdam/Barcroft Media; **35** (tr) Jim McAdam/Barcroft Media, (bl) Barcroft Media; **36** Christoph Rueegg/Alamy Stock Photo; **37** (bl) Courtesy of Berghotel Oeschinensee Familie Wandfluh; **38** (br) © Volodymyr Krasyuk/Shutterstock.com; **38–39** (t) KAREN MIKADO/CATERS NEWS; **39** (b) Paramount Group Anti-Poaching and K9 Academy/CATERS NEWS; **40–41** (bkg, tr) Instagram @Anonymouse_mmx; **41** (br) Tommy Lindholm/Pacific Press/LightRocket via Getty Images; **42–43** ASSOCIATED PRESS; **45** (cr) © David Aleksandrowicz/Shutterstock.com; **46** (br) TERRY TAYLOR/MERCURY PRESS; **46–47** (bkg) TERRY TAYLOR/CATERS NEWS; **47** (tr) © sanooker_seven/Shutterstock.com, (b) © george photo cm/Shutterstock.com; **48** (cl) © Chiradech Chotchuang/Shutterstock.com; **48–49** (bkg) Eugene Tang/Stockimo/Alamy Stock Photo; **52** (tl) © Vladimir Wrangel/Shutterstock.com, (tr) © AppStock/Shutterstock.com, (b) © Christopher Robin Smith Photography/Shutterstock.com; **53** (tl) © ArtHeart/Shutterstock.com, (tr) © michelangeloop/Shutterstock.com, (bl) © Kawin K/Shutterstock.com, (br) © Firuz Salamzadeh/Shutterstock.com; **54** (tr) © viktor_kov/Shutterstock.com, (bl) © User:Bdevel, Tyler from Seattle, WA, Wikimedia Commons // CC-BY-SA 3.0.; **54–55** (bkg) © xtrekx/Shutterstock.com, (bc) © Tikhonov/Shutterstock.com; **55** (tr) © Artem Shadrin/Shutterstock.com, (br) © ArtHeart/Shutterstock.com; **56** Els Van den Eijnden/Caters News; **57** (tr) Dr Carleton Ray via Getty Images, (br) © PavloArt Studio/Shutterstock.com; **58** (tr) © Jellis Vaes/Shutterstock.com; **60–61** Mark Conlin/Alamy Stock Photo; **62–63** Cynthia Delaney Suwito; **64** (cr) © Rvector/Shutterstock.com; **64–65** dpa picture alliance/Alamy Stock Photo; **65** (br) © SKARIDA/Shutterstock.com; **68** (t) De Klerk/Alamy Stock Photo, (br) © dnd_project/Shutterstock.com; **69** (tr) PA Images/Alamy Stock Photo, (br) James Boardman/Alamy Stock Photo; **70–71** Karwai Tang/WireImage; **72** (tl) © Peerapong W.Aussawa/Shutterstock.com, (cl) © cowardlion/Shutterstock.com, (cr) © MrNovel/Shutterstock.com, (bl) © MrNovel/Shutterstock.com, (br) © MrNovel/Shutterstock.com; **73** (tr) © livcool/Shutterstock.com; **74–75** Travel Pictures/Alamy Stock Photo; **75** (tr) © KNEFEL/Shutterstock.com, (br) © Sarawut Aiemsinsuk/Shutterstock.com; **76** (tr) © tanja-vashchuk/Shutterstock.com, (c) © Viktorija Reuta/Shutterstock.com, (br) © Nuamfolio/Shutterstock.com; **77** (t) © Gino Santa Maria/Shutterstock.com, (c) ACTIVE MUSEUM/Alamy Stock Photo, (b) © MARGRIT HIRSCH/Shutterstock.com; **78–79** REUTERS/Kim Kyung-Hoon; **80–81** © Nor Gal/Shutterstock.com; **82** (t) © Natalia van D/Shutterstock.com, (bl) Andrew Newman Nature Pictures/Alamy Stock Photo; **83** (tr) © fivespots/Shutterstock.com; **83** (br) blickwinkel/Alamy Stock Photo; **84–85** (bkg) Devin SuperTramp; **84** (br) © Sferdon/Shutterstock.com, (l) Public Domain {{PD-US}} NASA/http://www.nasa.gov/mission_pages/shuttle/behindscenes/Whatsgoingup.html, (bl) Public Domain {{PD-US}} NASA/https://www.nasa.gov/images/content/194007main_lightsaberpic.jpg; **86** (tr) © Public Domain {{PD-US}}, (c) © Petr Bukal/Shutterstock.com, (cl) © Fun Way Illustration/Shutterstock.com; **88** (t) © Debby Wong/Shutterstock.com, (cl, cr) © rvlsoft/Shutterstock.com, (br) © Rob Crandall/Shutterstock.com; **89** (t) © Tidarat Tiemjai/Shutterstock.com, (c) © pixinoo/Shutterstock.com, (br) AF archive/Alamy Stock Photo

Key: t = top, b = bottom, c = center, l = left, r = right, sp = single page, bkg = background

All other photos are from Ripley Entertainment Inc.

Every attempt has been made to acknowledge correctly and contact copyright holders, and we apologise in advance for any unintentional errors or omissions, which will be corrected in future editions.